**Books are to be returned on or before
the last date below.**

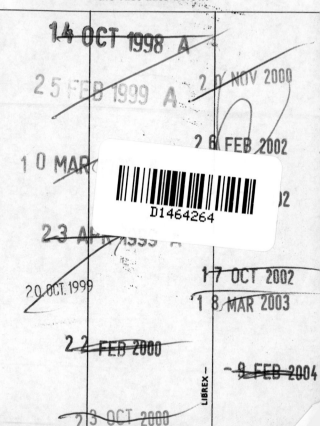

KIMONO

by Motoko Itô
&
Aiko Inoue

translated by
Patricia Massy

HOIKUSHA
保育社

CONTENTS

(Cover Photo)

A girl's *furisode* to be worn at weddings, New Year's festivities, parties, and other such felicitous occasions. The blue kimono is accented with a yellow extra collar called *date-eri*. A yellow *maru obi* interwoven with gold is tied at the back in a sumptuous bow.

KIMONO

by Motoko Itō & Aiko Inoue
translated by Patricia Massy

© All rights reserved. No.37 of Hoikusha's Color Books Series. Published by Hoikusha Publishing Co., Ltd., 8-6, 4-chome, Tsurumi, Tsurumi-ku, Osaka, 538 Japan. ISBN 4-586-54037-0. First Edition in 1979. 10th Edition in 1993. Printed in JAPAN

Kimono Today

Looking back to the time human beings began to clothe themselves, we find that irrespective of the geographical distinctions of east and west the first form of adornment was leaves. Narrow bands of cloth later came to be woven, followed by wider widths.

For instance, the ancient Egyptian costume was no more than a large cloth wrapped about the body. As the art of sewing was unknown, unlike modern western costume, the beauty of the outfit was simply in the harmonious fall of the cloth and the way it was draped. Likewise the Japanese costume developed from one piece of cloth. Undergoing early influences first from Korea and then T'ang China, it assumed Japanese characteristics during the classic Heian Period (794-1185) and has since been refined through the shifting trends of history to the form we know today.

Combining the various parts of kimono skillfully is an exercise in design. This is the joy of wearing kimono. It is not only the older generation that finds pleasure in this unique aspect of the Japanese costume.

Among the various types of kimono and materials, there are those that derive from ancient times and have become refined and perfected with the passing ages. Dyeing, weaving, and embroidery were not the work of some individual artist as were painting, sculpture or tea ceremony objects. Textiles grew among the common people, passing from the hands of one artisan to another. Through the fires of war, overcoming famines, these art forms have been bequeathed to us today.

While preserving the national costume of Japan and at the same time taking advantage of new synthetic materials, Japanese have kept the kimono as a vital part of modern life.

Types of Kimono

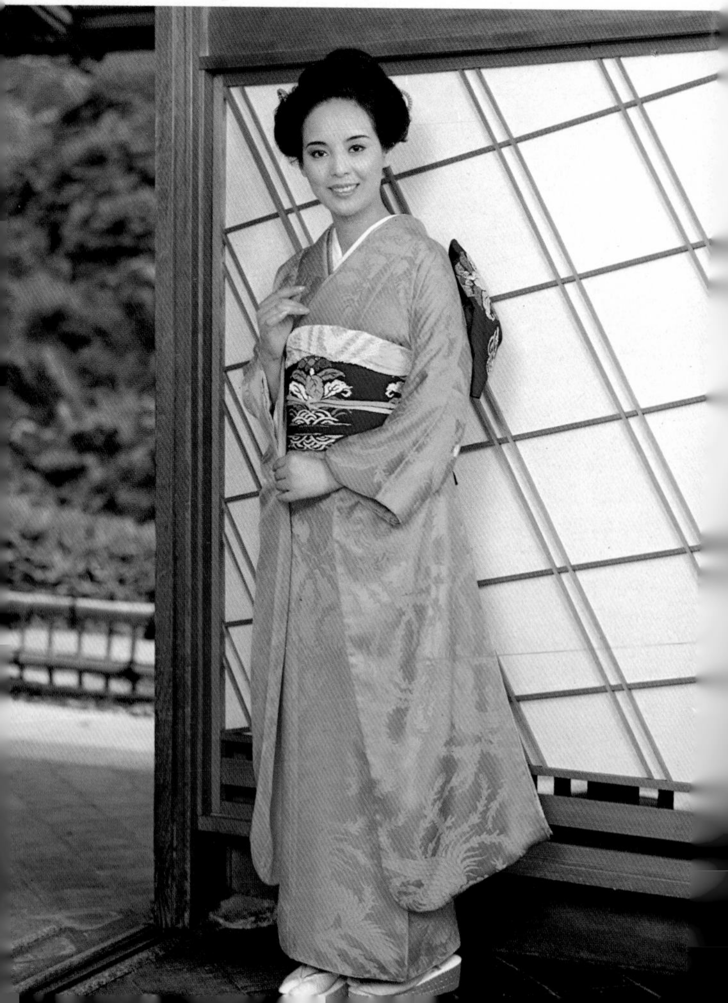

Furisode (Girl's Formal)

On the left-hand page a sophisticated *furisode* in a single hue demonstrates the beauty of layering. The vermillion kimono in figured satin is set against a green undergarment, a combination heightened by the dark purple *fukuro obi*.

The right-hand photo shows a satin *ôburisode* (*furisode* with full-length sleeves) on which have been employed the highest techniques of traditional textile decoration — hand painted *yûzen*, fine embroidery, and gold foil. The vermillion obi with a diamond design of pine needles in gold thread is a striking *maru obi*. The *obijime* (obi cord) in "young bamboo" color and the red *kanoko* tie-dye *obiage* (obi sash) provide a delightful girlish accent. The most elegant item of a girl's wardrobe, this outfit can be worn at a wedding or any formal social function.

3

Black Tomesode
(Woman's Formal)

The most formal attire for a married woman is the black *tomesode* with five crests. The contrasting white undergarment in *habutae* sharply defines the lines of the kimono. In the Kansai area this is made of crepe instead. The *fukuro obi* is given a full, sumptuous shape. The collar is white *shioze* silk, and the *obiage* white *kanoko* tie-dye or white figured satin. The *obijime* is either a white *maruguke* (cord of silk cloth) or a *kumihimo* (braided cord) in white, gold, or silver. The *zôri* also should be white or silver. The overall impression is of the finest elegance and refinement. Young women, however, may wear a pink *kanoko* tie-dye *obiage* and an undergarment of vermillion, red, or pink. Sometimes the collar of the undergarment is embroidered with silver thread.

Black Tomesode with Five Crests

Mofuku
(Mourning Apparel)

It is customary to wear a five-crested kimono in black *habutae* or *hitokoshi chirimen* crepe for mourning. All accessories including the sashes for tying the kimono must be black. The only exceptions are the collar, *tabi*, and undergarment, which are all white. In winter a lined kimono is worn, in summer *ro* gauze or an unlined outfit. It is also practical to have a black coat for such occasions.

Mourning Outfit
with Five Crests

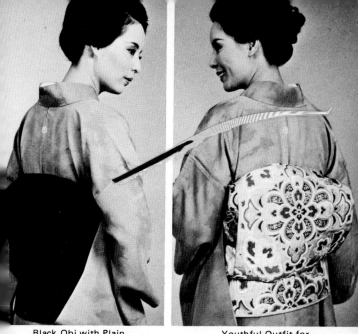

Black Obi with Plain
Kimono for Mourning

Youthful Outfit for
Social Gatherings

Muji Hitotsumon (Solid Color Kimono with One Crest)

For sheer practicality nothing equals a one-crested kimono in a single hue. It goes almost anywhere. Occasions of felicity and mourning, however, demand different colors and types of pattern in the figured cloth. Such motifs as tortoise shell octagons, waves, and fans go with bright colors. On the other hand, subdued tones and quiet colors are matched with clouds, water, leaves, or dots. At times of mourning the kimono and its accessories should be in the same color range.

9

Summer Town Wear and Hômongi

The left-hand kimono for town wear is of Satsuma ramie, one of the most luxurious of summer materials. It is matched with an unlined *nagoya obi* in *ro* gauze that has a tapestry design at the back.

The embroidery of autumn grasses upon the black gauze of the *hômongi* on the right creates an aura of poetic refinement. It is worn with an unlined *ro* gauze obi decorated with tapestry designs. Within the fan designs are accents of embroidery.

Summer Hômongi

A *ro* gauze *hômongi* decorated with hand-painted western flowers. The unlined obi is of *ro* gauze with a tapestry design.

11

Summer Fabrics

Kimono materials may be broadly classified as either white undyed cloth or weaves made of dyed yarns such as *Ôshima* or *omeshi*. As there are altogether many varieties, here only the undyed cloth will be taken up for detailed explanation.

Winter materials include *chirimen* (crepe) with such names as *kodai chirimen* or *hitokoshi chirimen*, figured satin weaves such as *hira rinzu* and *koma rinzu*, embroidery weave, *habutae* (plain silk), *koma muji* (silk with a highly twisted yarn), *jôdai* (combination reeled silk and spun silk yarns), and *Yûki* (hand-spun silk). Of these the following are worn unlined from the end of May to the middle of June: *hitokoshi, habutae, koma muji, jôdai,* and *Yûki*.

For summertime *ro* gauze, *sha* gauze, and ramie help to relieve the heat. Both warp and weft *ro* are made; in other words, the mesh pattern runs either vertically or horizontally. While unfigured *ro* is reserved for formal wear for men and women, figured *ro* is considered appropriate for women's *hômongi* and *komon*. Another *ro* variant that is used for women's *hômongi* or *komon* is made of highly twisted yarn. It is called *koma ro*. Depending on the size of the mesh, there are several grades of *ro* from fine to rough. The latter are for obi, *obiage*, and collars. *Ro* is worn from the end of June to the beginning of September.

Transparent *sha* is popular at the height of summer. It is for men's black *haori* and women's dyed *hômongi*. *Sha* with a patterned weave is made into women's *haori, hômongi, tsukesage*, solid color crested kimono, and undergarments for summer wear. Figured *sha* in a multicolored weave is worn for visiting wear, *haori*, and summer coats.

Ramie is also worn during the hottest months. It is used for men's *montsuki*, women's colored *tomesode*, *hômongi*, solid color crested kimono, and as a ground for *yûzen* painting and *komon* stencil designs. Undergarments are made of ramie woven with transparent patterns. Plain ramie and rough ramie *ro* gauze are made up into *nagoya obi*. There are many other varieties of ramie as well.

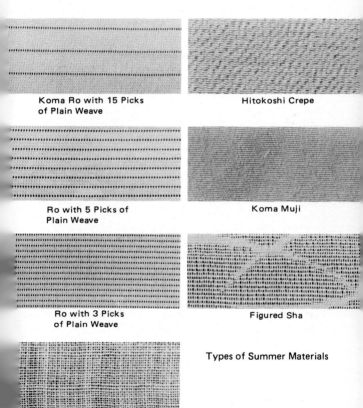

Koma Ro with 15 Picks
of Plain Weave

Hitokoshi Crepe

Ro with 5 Picks of
Plain Weave

Koma Muji

Ro with 3 Picks
of Plain Weave

Figured Sha

Types of Summer Materials

Ramie

Summer Town Wear

On the left, *yûzen koma ro* gauze; on the right, *ojiya chijimi* kimono for high summer worn with a *nagoya obi*. The *obijime* is a thin summer type braided cord.

Yukata (Cotton Prints for Casual Wear)

Crisp and cool, that is how a *yukata* should look; never untidy. See pages 84-89 for instructions on putting it on.

Haori Jackets

No matter how expensive a *haori* may be, it is only for informal wear and inappropriate for tea gatherings or formal occasions. A black or pastel crested *haori* is slightly dressy while hand-painted designs, *sarasa* (chintz type printed designs), and stencil designs are worn for going into town or casually visiting friends. *Kasuri* weaves in silk or cotton are often made into kimono-*haori* ensembles. Also, a practical addition for home wear is the *chabaori*. Made of softly woven wool or a knit, it presents a good opportunity to play with interesting colors and materials. It is important to remember that the length of the *haori* and the sleeves differ according to the type of kimono with which it is worn. The person's height must also be taken into consideration, and the *haori* cords have to match the *haori* in value.

Haori for Wearing
in Town

Ensemble of Kurume
Cotton Kasuri Both for
Town and Home

A wool knit chabaori
makes a warm house
jacket.

Coats

Coats come in three lengths: full-length, three-quarter, and short. The coat on the left is a reproduction of a period fabric cut in the style of a Noh play costume. The red cords add a touch of luxury. Immediately one knows that it must have come from the skilled hands of Kyoto weavers. On the right is the type of coat called *michiyuki*. Dyed in a design of scattered pieces of colored paper, it can be worn over *hômongi* or *tsukesage*. Besides these examples, there are also coats made of stenciled patterns, printed patterns, batik, tie-dye, spun silk, *kasuri*, wool, and velvet. When choosing a coat, one must keep the style and value of the kimono in mind.

18

Men's Kimono

Lately men have shown a new interest in wearing kimono. Especially popular are the New Year's elegant *haori* style and *yukata* for summer festivals. Men's formal kimono are the five-crested black *habutae haori* with *hakama* and the light colored three-crested *habutae haori*. For informal wear there are *Yûki*, *Ôshima*, solid color *tsumugi*, *omeshi*, *habutae*, and the very casual Kurume *kasuri*. In summer a black plain *ro* gauze *haori* with five crests is worn with *hakama* in *ro* gauze or *sha* gauze. An alternative is a three-crested *haori* in light colored plain *ro* gauze or linen. Other summer fabrics are Echigo ramie, Satsuma ramie, *Yûki* crepe, *Yûki*, Kurume *kasuri*, and the cotton *yukata*. The undergarment, footwear, coat, and *haori* must all be co-ordinated in the same manner as a woman's outfit.

Although colors are predominately dark and subdued, such as umber, grey, or blue, age determines the intensity of color, size of pattern, and quality. For instance, a boy will wear a Kurume *kasuri* with a large pattern while a smaller pattern would be suitable for a middle-aged man. Also silk *Ôshima* or *Yûki* would be inappropriate before a person had attained a mature appearance.

For one's first outfit, a kimono-*haori* ensemble in wool *Ôshima* or Kurume *kasuri* is an inexpensive and practical choice. A *keisô obi* tied in a bow will avoid the difficulties of tying posed by a stiff *kaku obi*. A *nagajuban* (full-length undergarment) of cotton flannel, muslin, or synthetic material will do, and underneath it a plain cotton *hadagi* (undershirt). Both should have a collar in either black or dark blue. Instead of the *hadagi*, a V-neck short sleeved undershirt may be worn, but underwear that is visible at the ankle is to be avoided. Dark blue is a good color to choose for the *tabi*. Anyone who is wearing kimono for the first time is recommended to first practice putting on the *tabi* and walking and sitting in kimono. The *haori* and kimono do not need to be of the same material so long as the combination is in good taste. Under an *Ôshima* or *Yûki* kimono for visiting, a *nagajuban* in *habutae, tsumugi*, crepe, or Fuji silk is worn. The *haori* of *habutae* has a single crest embroidered on the back. There are also *haori* of *tsumugi* or *omeshi* in a solid color.

Black Habutae Haori
with Hakama

Wool Ensemble for
Everyday Wear in
Two-tone Indigo Kasuri·

Kimono and Haori
in Indigo Ôshima
for Going Out

22

Yukata with Keisô Obi and Boy's
Happi for a Summer Festival

Kimono Fabrics and Patterns

Ôshima Tsumugi

It is said that one day a girl on the island of Amami Ôshima left her washing in the paddy water. When she returned the next day and took the kimono from out of the mud, she was surprised to find that it had become a pleasant brown color. It was such an attractive color that the next time she wove a kimono, she first dyed the yarn in the mud. It turned out to be an extraordinarily beautiful material.

The silk yarn of *Ôshima tsumugi* is dyed with the techi tree (*Rhaphiolepis umbellata* var. *Mertensii*). The bark, which has strong tannic acid, is chopped up with a hatchet and then boiled. Into this extract the yarn is submerged altogether ten times. Slowly it takes on a red hue and then darkens into brown. The dyed yarn is now dumped into a mud bath. Time and again it is rubbed into the mud. Because the iron in the mud is what sets the color of the dye, after about a month of use, the mud has lost all its iron content and a new plot of mud must be made. As new mud is constantly required, the hillsides have become terraced with muddy ponds like the one shown in the photograph.

This dyeing technique is said to defy immitation because nowhere else is there as much iron in the soil as on Amami Ôshima. The weaving also is a time-consuming task. More than a month is needed to complete a length for one kimono.

Wood of the Techi Tree

Mud Dyeing

Tsumugi (Spun Silk)

Made throughout Japan, *tsumugi* has a rustic, hand-made flavor that has placed it among the most popular of kimono fabrics. The left photo on the right-hand page shows an unlined kimono. Its pattern of hemp leaves on a white background gives it an air of coolness. It is to be worn for casual occasions. Traditionally a dyed obi is combined with a woven kimono, but a woven obi has purposely been chosen for the right-hand kimono on the facing page. Its woven design resembles an oil painting.

A dyed obi in ribbed weave adds softness to a kimono of Ōshima tsumugi.

Unlined Tsumugi   Lined Tsumugi

Omeshi Chirimen (Heavy Crepe)

Because *omeshi* lies neatly and gives a smart figure, it is highly recommendable for anyone who is wearing kimono for the first time. The usual patterns are stripes and *kasuri*.

The weft yarn is twisted both left and right and woven two together. In brief, *omeshi* is produced as follows. First of all, the skein of raw silk is boiled in a cauldron of water until soft. After it has been dried, it is draped over a bamboo pole and submerged in the dye vat. Holding either end of the pole, two men turn the yarn over the pole and watch the progress of the dyeing. The weft yarn is then waxed.

If the pattern is to be *kasuri*, the dyed yarn is tied here and there at predetermined points with rubber strips and dyed. Wherever it has been tied, the yarn retains the color of the first dye bath. Later the yarn is twisted. The degree of twisting will determine the weight of the crepe.

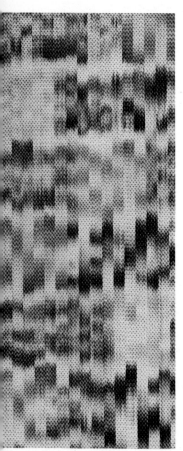

Hand-woven Omeshi Kasuri

Omeshi with
Pink and Black
Stripes

Yarn Tied with
Rubber Strips for
Kasuri Dyeing

Two Types of Omeshi

A Kimono of True Kihachijô

Kihachijô (Yellow Plaid)

The hand-woven cloth of Hachijô Island boasts of a history as long as that of Kurume *kasuri*. Its extraordinary yellow comes from a dye made of the *kariyasu* grass that thrives on the island. Although true *kihachijô* cloth has become rare, lately the same patterns and colors are being reproduced in wool at the town of Isezaki. This new material is also very popular.

Komon (Overall Pattern)

Any material covered completely with the same stencil or batik pattern is called *komon*. While Kyoto was famous for hand-painted designs, *komon* was popular in Edo, and so it is also known as *Edo komon*.

Komon patterns are carved with painstaking patience and fine skill from paper stencils. The material that is to be patterned is pasted on a long board, and a resist of rice paste is spread through the stencil onto the cloth. When the pattern has been applied to the whole cloth, the background is covered with resist containing the ground dye. Care must be taken that the stencil never moves while the resist is being applied and that the pattern is laid straight. It certainly is not work that can be learned overnight. Many long years of training are required before an artisan can apply the resist successfully.

As it is one of the traditional types of kimono, *komon* can be seen in Kabuki and Bunraku costumes. It is said to have developed from the dyed designs of the samurai's formal costume of Edo Period. From one to three colors are used.

Recently a fine pattern called *same* (sharkskin) *komon* has gained favor. If this is decorated with a crest at the back, it can be worn like *hômongi* for dress-up occasions.

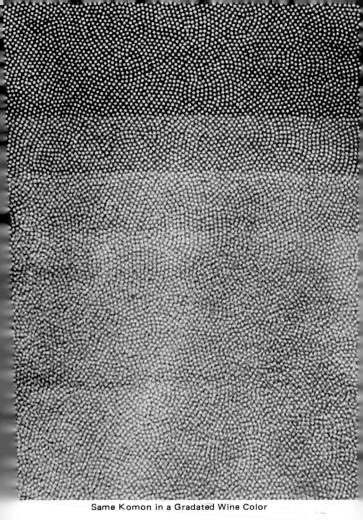

Same Komon in a Gradated Wine Color

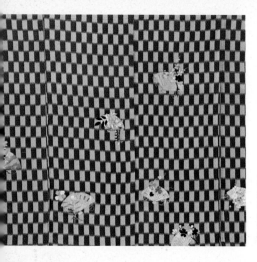

Crepe Komon
with
Embroidered Fans
Scattered over
the Checkerboard
Pattern

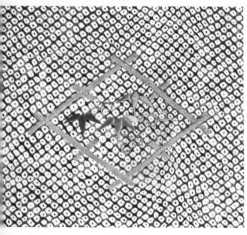

Embroidered
Komon of
Figured Satin
Printed in
Imitation
Tie-dye

Crepe Komon

Shibori (Tie-Dye)

Tie-dyeing is employed not only for formal attire such as *montsuki* or *hômongi*, but also for simple obi worn by men and children. On a hot summer's day nothing feels quite as refreshing as a *shibori yukata*. In the Shôsôin Imperial Repository of 8th century artifacts, there is a remnant of *shibori* dyeing, attesting to the fact that this technique has been loved by the Japanese since ancient times.

Shibori may be machine-made as are the *yukata* designs or hand-made. The latter demands, or course, a high price since it is such tedious work. The most elaborate example is the polka dot pattern called *kanoko shibori*. Each dot has to be tied tightly with fine silk thread, and 300,000 of these dots may go into a kimono completely covered with *shibori*. Even in this age of advanced technology such indescribable beauty can be achieved only with the human hands. Today the exacting work of *shibori* dyeing is carried out in the Arimatsu Narumi area of Aichi Prefecture and in part of Kyoto Prefecture.

Shibori and Yûzen on Hômongi

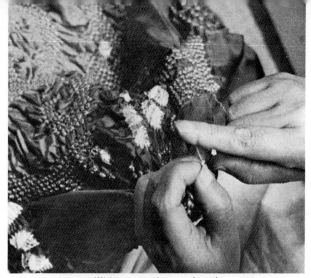

With one continuous thread
the shibori tufts are tyed.

The tie-dye *furisode* displayed on the kimono rack is the work of Zenichirô Ueda. Having devoted a lifetime to the improvement of Kyoto's textile industry, he is an advisor to the Kyoto Tie-Dye Guild and a committeeman of the dyeing and embroidery section of the Kyoto Prefectural Industrial Arts Research Association.

The photograph below shows a detail of another one of the kimono produced by Ueda's workshop, Ueda Zen, Co., Ltd. Both kimono are superb examples of how tie-dye, embroidery and hand-dyeing are combined to form luxurious works of textile art.

Yûzen (Hand-Painted Patterns)

Regarded as representative of Japanese kimono design, *yûzen* is said to have originated in the Genroku Era (1688-1704) of the Edo Period. Supposedly its creator was a Kyoto designer by the name of Miyazaki Yûzen, but the truth of the story is lost in the foggy past. Although *yûzen* was popularized in Kyoto, it also came to be produced in Kaga, present-day Ishikawa Prefecture. Kyoto *yûzen* and Kaga *yûzen* display individual styles of design and coloring, yet both are based on the same fundamental techniques.

As the fabric changes and develops in the dyeing process numerous steps are involved. The most common method is to transfer the design to the kimono with a delible ink made from the dayflower called *aobana*. When the fabric is later washed, this ground sketch will disappear. The areas to be dyed are outlined with resist made from rice paste so that the dye will not bleed into the background. The resist is applied by squeezing it from a tube with a pointed spout. After the colors have been placed within the outlines, the whole bolt is steamed. The steaming process improves the color of the fabric and sets the dyed areas. Now the colored parts are all covered with resist, and the background dye is applied with a wide brush. Because the design is protected by the resist, it will not be damaged. Again the fabric is steamed, but this time it is washed out afterwards. It is then sent to be stretched and evened up. In former days *yûzen*-dyed fabric was washed in the Kamo River in Kyoto. The long strips of brightly dyed cloth waving in the clear current were one of the unforgettable sights of Kyoto.

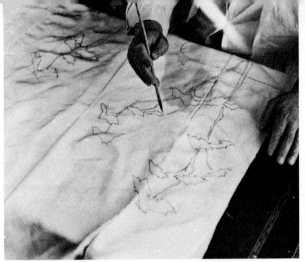

Sketching the Design in Delible Ink

Outlining the Areas to be Dyed with Resist

Applying the Dye

Yûki
Tsumugi

Yûki Tsumugi (Hand-spun Silk)

True *Yûki tsumugi* comes from the city of Yûki in Ibaragi Prefecture. Since the 14th century this fabric was presented to the central feudal government by the Yûki Clan, and thus it came to be known by that name. Like *Ôshima tsumugi*, it is not acceptable for formal wear despite its high price. Another characteristic is its durable, strong thread which becomes ever more beautiful and soft the longer it is worn. That *Yûki tsumugi* should fray or tear is unheard of.

It is woven into either a plain tabby or a crepe, the former being designated an Intangible Cultural Asset. From the spinning of the yarn to the *kasuri* weaving, this difficult textile demands great patience and long hours of work. The weft yarn of the crepe weave is given a crepe twist as in *chirimen* crepe.

To complete one bolt with a fine design may require as much as a year. The yarn is taken from inferior cocoons that have been boiled with caustic soda, soaked in water, and then stretched into bag-like squares. After the silk squares have been thoroughly dried, the silk thread is spun from them. This is a painstaking task. Even an experienced person spends about 30 days spinning enough for one kimono. Later the yarn must be bound to make the *kasuri* patterns. Whether the *kasuri* will be poor or excellent depends on the quality of this basic step.

Yûki Woven at Ishige

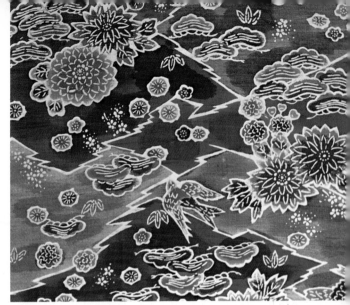

above: Dress-up Kimono of Spun Silk Dyed in Bingata Designs
below: Bingata on Cotton

(left) Hōmongi of Figured Satin
Dyed with a Bingata Design

Bingata (Okinawan Designs)

Okinawa is the home of *bingata*, a dyeing technique with a long tradition. Most *bingata* designs are stenciled and usually occur on ramie or cotton. Dating back 300 or so years, *bingata* was originally reserved for the Okinawan nobility. Later it spread to the general populace and today is a favorite among all the people of Japan.

The *bin* of *bingata* literally means crimson in Japanese. It seems to have been chosen, however, to indicate that brilliant colors are employed. *Kata* is stencil; yet the resist trailing technique also falls in the *bingata* category.

Okinawan prints have an extraordinary freedom that flows even through the stencil designs. Such abandonment in stencil techniques must be unique in the world of textiles. The use of a single stencil has been preserved faithfully through the centuries, and it has proved a highly effective means of bringing a design to life. All sorts of colors in natural dyes are used: white, yellow, red, violet, purple, indigo, turquoise. The crimson is especially attractive. *Bingata* truly captures the brilliance and warmth of the south, but the designs of plants, animals, houses, boats, fans, and the like are objects close to everyday life on all the Japanese islands.

Bingata on Ramie

Tôkamachi Silk

During the winter Niigata Prefecture is blanketed in snow. In the Tôkamachi area where the snow is particularly deep, the endurance of the people in overcoming the rigors of this severe climate has produced a unique textile that has been known since the 7th century. With hands chilled by the frosty air, steadfastly they have spun the silk yarn, dyed it, and then woven it into kimono fabric. Because Tôkamachi is on a plain that is surrounded by mountains on four sides and has abundant precipitation, the degree of humidity remains more or less stable day and night. This is an ideal condition for the spinning and weaving of silk and ramie and no doubt influenced the growth of the textile industry there.

Tôkamachi Kasuri

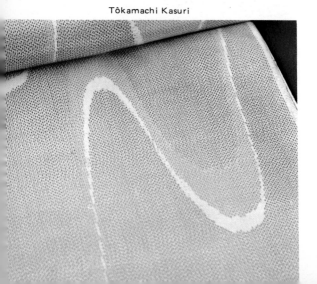

Akanezome

Akanezome (Madder)

Both madder and *murasaki*, a variety of gromwell that gives a deep purple, are specialities of Iwate Prefecture where these two plants grow indigenously. The dye is taken from the roots, and over a period of many months it is applied to the yarn with the aid of a mordant made of wood ash.

Japanese people long ago believed that these dyes would protect them from illness. Woven into a *tsumugi* type material, madder and gromwell are always pleasant to wear, and they retain a soft color.

Jacquard

Whenever kimono or obi fabrics are woven on power looms, the Jacquard system is employed. With every throw of the shuttle, the system automatically changes and thus it is possible to carry out the most involved patterns. First of all, the pattern must be worked out on graph paper. As each block represents an intersection of the warp and weft threads, the graph immediately indicates the exact color and placement of the yarns.

Next the pattern is punched out on paper cards. These are

Nishijin Power Looms at Work

strung together into a belt and fitted onto the mechanism of the Jacquard loom.

Invented by a Frenchman by the name of Joseph Marie Jacquard, this system revolutionized weaving. In the late 19th century, three Nishijin experts brought the Jacquard loom to Japan after a year's study in France where they had been sent by the governor of Kyoto. To the north of the present Kyoto Hotel in the Kawaramachi district of Kyoto, they built a weaving center. Students from all over Japan flocked there to learn the Jacquard weave. A monument now stands on the site.

Jacquard Obi and Its Graphed Design

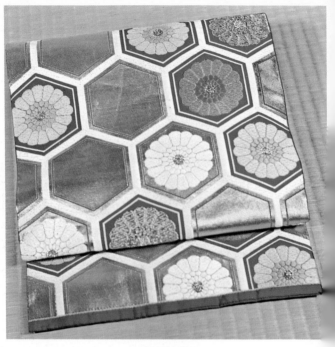

Nishiki Obi

Types of Obi

Nishiki (Brocade) Obi

The most elegant obi are of brocade. Woven by hand with utmost care, brocade is a sumptuous fabric making use of gold and silver thread. The usual patterns depict flowers or birds, or are taken from ancient geometrical designs. As almost all

Nishiki Obi

brocade comes from the Nishijin district of Kyoto, it is commonly called "*Nishijin obi* material." This brocade is woven into *maru obi* for bridal outfits, *fukuro obi* or *nagoya obi*. The weft may be made entirely of gold or silver foil which must be inserted into the weave one strip at a time with a bamboo rod so that it will not twist.

Tsuzure (Tapestry) Obi

Worn at such dress-up occasions as weddings, tapestry obi are the ultimate in luxury. Not only at home, but also abroad, the dexterity of Japanese tapestry weavers is acclaimed, and the opulent products of their hands are as renowned as those of the Gobelin works. The stunning stage curtains in Japanese theaters are also among the masterpieces they create.

Tapestry is said to have been born in Babylon. That it was known in Japan some 1,300 years ago is documented by the magnificent examples in the Shôsôin Imperial Repository in Nara.

Although most weaving has now become mechanized,

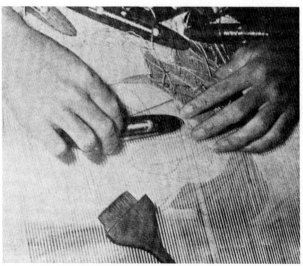

Patiently the tapestry is woven.

tapestry still depends on the fingernails of the weaver. The design is drawn on tracing paper, then transferred in reverse to another sheet on which the colors are worked out. This is placed directly under the warp of the loom so that the weaver can weave in the colors exactly as they appear on the draft below. Each color is worked with a separate shuttle. The weaver compacts the yarn into the weave by raking it with the fingernails. To do this work effectively, the nails are allowed to grow and are filed like the zig-zag teeth of a saw. Thus they act in the same manner as a comb. Primitive though this technique may be, it is essential for tapestry weaving.

Saw-Toothed Nails

Finished Piece

Fukuro Obi of Rayon and Silk

The pictured *fukuro obi* is of damask weave with a warp of rayon and a weft of silk. Although it has the appearance of pure silk, it costs only about half as much, an important factor to consider for one's first *fukuro obi*. Synthetic fibers, however, give less volume to the bow, and metallic foil lacks the luster of true gold.

Fukuro Obi ⇨
of
Rayon and Silk

⇦ (left)
Tapestry Maru Obi

Synthetic Silk Nagoya Obi

This red satin obi with silver and gold embroidery is so well-made that only a specialist could tell whether it is silk or synthetic. Being entirely of synthetic fiber, it feels rather heavy when worn and the colors lack subtle nuances. On the other hand, such an obi can be had for one-third to one-fourth the price of a silk piece. It also is easy to sew. For casual wear, a synthetic obi should be quite practical.

Embroidered Obi

As beautiful as *yûzen* or *komon* kimono may be just as they are, adding a touch of gold and silver embroidery accentuates and glorifies the design. (See p. 34)

Nowadays machine embroidered obi are made for *hômongi* and the like. Needless to say, handwork is more likely to convey truly graceful elegance, and it will last much longer.

Figured Satin with Embroidery

Hakata Obi

Hakata weaving was begun by a man called Yasôemon Mitsuda about 700 years ago during the reign of Emperor Shijô. For six long years he had stayed in China studying textiles. Upon his return, he succeeded to the family weaving works and later sent his own children abroad for further learning. Their combined efforts gave rise to this famed weave.

Hakata Fukuro Obi

Hakata Kenjô

The *Hakata obi* of today are the legacy of their trials and perseverance.

Hakata is commonly called *kenjô*, which means tribute, because starting in 1600 the local daimyo, Kuroda Nagamasa, had *Hakata obi* sent to the shogunate. This tribute was presented every year in March. "Five Colored *Kenjô*" symbolizes the five virtues that are said to have been learned from the precepts of Sui Dynasty China, namely purple: virtue, red: propriety, yellow: sincerity, blue: wisdom, and green: humanity.

Hakata obi used to be mostly simple summer obi, but now *fukuro obi* and *nagoya obi* for winter use are also popular.

How To Wear Kimono

On Wearing Kimono

In recent years it has become quite easy to learn how to put on kimono because all sorts of magazines give pointers on the subject and schools devoted to the apparel of kimono have sprung up. In order not to forget what one has gone to the trouble to learn, it is important to take every opportunity to put the lessons to practice and get accustomed to handling kimono by oneself.

The procedures explained here will serve for any occasion. Though modernized, they are basically the same as those employed in the past. To look elegant the following 8 points must be remembered.

1. Wear kimono that fit your proportions. (This includes *nagajuban* and obi.)
2. Pay attention to the type of material. (For instance, *nagajuban* should be chosen according to the weight and texture of the kimono.)
3. Choose good material. (If an unlined narrow obi is of synthetic fiber, it often is too slippery, causing the knot to loosen and the obi to sag.)
4. Have all neccessary accessories.
5. Know your physical characteristics.
6. Arrange your hair to harmonize with kimono. (The nape of the neck is the glamor spot of kimono.)
7. Choose accessories that match the outfit in character, color, pattern, and value.
8. Take proper care of the kimono after it has been worn.

With these points in mind, you are ready to take your first step.

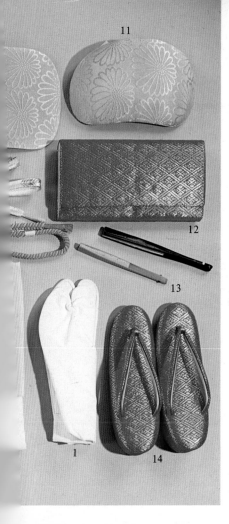

Accessories
for
Formal Kimono

1. *Tabi*
2. *Hadagi*
   (Undershirt)
3. *Susoyoke*
   (Underskirt)
4. *Datemaki*
5. *Koshi Himo*—
   at least 5
   sashes
6. *Koshi
   Makura*
   (Waist Pad)
7. *Obidomegane*
   (Obi clip)
8. *Obiage*
9. Obi *Mae-ita*
   (Obi Board)
10. *Obijime*
11. *Obiage Shin*
    (Bow Pad)
12. Handbag
13. Fan
14. *Zôri*
    (The *zôri*
    and hand-
    bag do not
    need to
    match, but
    they must be
    of equal value.)

How to Put On Furisode and Hômongi
1. The *nagajuban* is put on over the underclothes.
2. Tie the sash at the middle. Wrapping it around the chest only one time will avoid a double thickness, but it might be wise for those unaccustomed to kimono to wrap the sash twice. Be careful not to tie it too tightly or it will be uncomfortable. As in Fig. 1, sewing the sash to the *nagajuban* holds the collar and shoulders neatly in place. Usually muslin in pastel colors is used for the sashes.
3. Should the *nagajuban* be too long, it can be shortened as in Fig. 3, or it can be sewn down at the waist.

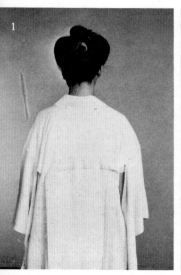

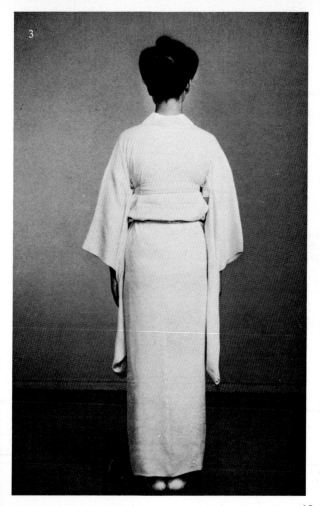

4. The *datemaki* is wrapped around the body from the chest down to the waist.
5. The collar of the *nagajuban* forms the foundation for the kimono, and therefore it should be firm. A soft collar should be provided with a stiffener inside.
6. Put on the kimono and align the hem. Decide on the width of the front panel of the skirt. Without losing this measurement, open the kimono and bring the right-hand side forward.

7. Walking is facilitated by folding the extra material of the inside panel forward. Also both the corners of the hem are raised. If the inside is raised 5 centimeters, the outside is also raised 5 cm. The hem at the back should barely touch the floor. Whenever the *zôri* will not be taken off, such as at hotel receptions, the kimono is worn slightly longer to compensate for the height of the *zôri*.

8.9. Wrap a sash twice around the waist just above the hip bone; tie in a bow or simply twist the ends under the sash. Make sure the ends are tidily tucked away so they won't show.

10. Put the hand through the opening under the left sleeve and straighten out the lower bodice.

11.12. When the inside has been put in order, place the left front over it and neatly arrange the line of the collar.

13. Once the bodice has been so arranged that it will remain in place, a sash is tied under the breast. Holding the sash in both hands, press it against the kimono in front and then, still pulling tightly, slip the hands around to the back. Cross the sash and tie it in front.

14. Coax the folds at the front and back of the bodice to the sides and smooth out the material. This gives room to lift the arms without tugging and putting the kimono in disarray.

74

15

16

15. Should the doubled over part around the waist be too long, it can be raised and the extra portion tucked as flat as possible under the waist sash. About 5 to 7 centimeters should show below the obi. Now a *datemaki* is tied around the waist. Be careful that it is no wider than the obi or it will show.

16. Because the obi is placed directly over it, the *datemaki* serves as a foundation and it should be given as much width as possible.

17.18. Once the *datemaki* has been tied, the kimono is
all ready. As shown in Fig. 15, extra material in the
doubled over part is tucked under the sash equally at
the front and back to produce a neat, pleasing
appearance. The length is determined by the person's
height. The *datemaki* holds the armholes firmly in place
and is a foundation for the obi. The best choice is
Hakata datemaki because it is strong and lies flat.

19. Now the obi is put on. For this *chûburisode*, a *fukuro
obi* has been chosen and it is to be tied in an *oshidori*,
mandarin duck, bow. With the short end of the obi at

19

the back of the right shoulder, bring the trailing end to the right and wrap it around the waist twice. The second time around, the point where the pattern starts should come at the right side just past the middle of the back. The short end should be just long enough for the tip to be hidden in the finished bow. Young people wear the obi rather wide, and so it is folded two-thirds its width instead of one-half. The width is judged by eye according to the person's height. If the pattern at the other end of the obi is easier to arrange, the obi can be wrapped from the left as well as from the right.

20

21

22

20. After the obi has been brought around to the front, the obi board is sandwiched behind it.

21. The obi is wrapped around to the back, and the short end is brought down to the left over it. The two are held by an obi clip. The larger the clip the better.

22. The waist pad is attached to the bottom of the clip. The strings are tied at the front and tucked under the obi.

23. To tie the mandarin duck bow, first of all the short end is formed into a loop and given a few pleats. This is held temporarily by a sash that is tied in front.

24. Now the long end is arranged the same way. Because the reverse side of a *fukuro obi* is always plain, the wings have to be looped, rather than folded back.

25. The right-hand wing is also pleated at the side of the clip and held by the temporary sash.

26. The two wings completed.
27. Next comes the body. Make a box pleat at the top as shown in the photo and drape it over the bow pad. In this step, it is important to study the pattern of the obi and work out an artistic placement of the design.
28. The obi and the bow pad underneath it should rest securely on the clip. If the pad falls off the clip, the whole arrangement will sag. Use a thick pad. The strings cross over the obi wings, thus holding them in place, and are tied in front.
29. Remove the temporary sash.

28

29

30. The tying of the obi is now completed. As in the photo, it should be well balanced and shaped. A *kanoko* tie-dye *obiage* conceals the bow pad. Fasten it securely at the front.

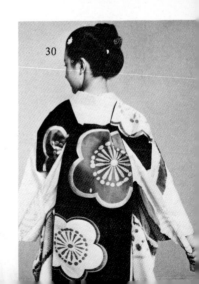

30

31

32

33

31. Instead of being tied, the *obiage* is tucked over the edge of the obi, first the right side, then the left over it. A nice border is a girlish accent and lends a dash of color as well.

32. 33. The dangling end of the obi is folded under, and an *obijime* is passed over it. The *obijime* is tied at the middle of the front. The mandarin duck bow is now finished.

Front and Rear View of the Completed Outfit

How to Put On Yukata

Kimono are usually raised at the waist and held with a sash, but if this is inconvenient, the tuck can be sewn in place or the kimono can be made to fit your height as are men's kimono. Traditional narrow width obi can be tied in any number of ways — enjoy inventing your own if you like.

⇩1. 2. Choose the width of the front panel and, without losing this measurement, wrap the left side over the right. The surplus cloth on the right-hand panel is folded forward.

⇦⇧1. The waist tuck has been sewn in place, and a sash has been sewn to both the left and right-hand edges.
  2. The sashes are crossed at the back and tied in front.
  3. Hold about 45cm of obi in the left hand; the rest in the right.

⇩3. Fasten kimono at waist with a sash.
  4. Put hand through armhole and straighten lower bodice.
  5. Arrange collar; tie bodice with a sash.

⇧4. Wrap long end around the waist twice.
5. Tie. The short end should be on top.

⇩6. Take 50-60cm of obi in the left hand.
7. Wrap obi twice around the waist.

6. 7. Pull long end to the right and fold to width of waist with the knot forming the center.

8. Fold short end in half lengthwise and tie.
9. The long end at the upper left is brought to the right.

8. Hold middle of bow with the left hand and short end with the right.
9. Bring short end around bow.

10. Accordian-pleat long end four times to width of waist.
11. 12. Make two deep ridges in middle of bow, bring short end up and around bow. Tie, bring end around again, and tuck surplus behind obi. Spread the bow. ⇨

⇧10. Knot by pulling end through to upper left.
11. Holding knot with right hand, pull obi towards the right. Straighten the arrangement. This bow is called "*ichimoji kuzushi.*"

⇩13. Holding knot, slip obi to the right.
14. Straighten bow. This butterfly bow is called "*chô musubi.*"

Drum Bow for Tsukesage and Komon

1. The *otaiko,* or drum, bow made with a *fukuro nagoya obi* is tied in the following manner. Start with the narrow (plain end) end of the obi at the back of the right shoulder and bring the trailing end to the right around the waist. Wrap it twice, inserting the obi board the second time around.

2. Drop the short end that is at the right shoulder, bringing it to the lower left, and insert the obi clip.

3. After pulling both ends tight, lock the clip.

4. The waist pad is put over the clip. The strings are tied in front and tucked under the obi.

5. Looking in the mirror, arrange the material so that the pattern will appear on the "drum" part. Put the bow pad under the peak of the obi and rest it in a steady position on the obi clip. Before tying the strings in front, shape the peak of the obi however you wish.

7

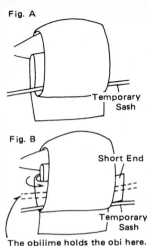

Fig. A

Temporary Sash

Fig. B

Short End

Temporary Sash

The obijime holds the obi here.

6. When the strings of the bow pad have been tied and tucked under the obi, the ends of the *obiage* are neatly folded, tied, and prettily tucked into the obi at the left and right sides.

7. There are various ways of arranging the *obiage,* but for *tsukesage* or *komon* outfits, to reveal only a discreet amount is more alluring than to show too much.

8. Shape the drum part of the obi and insert the short end. To accomplish this in one go is difficult for a novice. In this case it is helpful to first hold the drum part with a temporary sash passed through the loop at the lowest point as in Fig. A. With the obi thus held securely, the short end can be easily put in place. Adjust the length as neccessary. After the *obijime* has been tied, take the temporary sash off as in Fig. B.

8

9. When the obi is in order, pass the *obijime* through the loop of the drum.

10. Center the *obijime*, tie securely and tuck the two ends under either side of the cord.

11. The finished *otaiko* bow. The younger the person, the longer the end that shows at the bottom.

Accessories for Tsukesage and Komon

As these kimono can be worn at various types of occasions, accessories should be chosen appropriately for the event. The handbag and *zôri* need not match so long as they are similar in character.

11

Accessories below: 1.2. Leather Handbag and *Zôri*, 3.4. Beaded Handbag and *Zôri*, 5. Tea Ceremony Fan, 6. Three Types of *Obiage*, 7. *Obijime*, 8. Waist Pad, 9. Bow Pad for Young Women, 10. Bow Pad for Older Women, 11. Obi Clip, 12. Obi Board, 13. Undershirt, 14. Underskirt, 15. *Tabi*, 16. Sashes, 17. *Datejime* and *Datemaki*

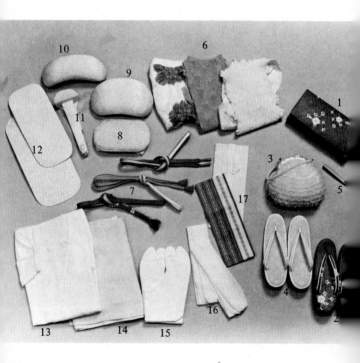

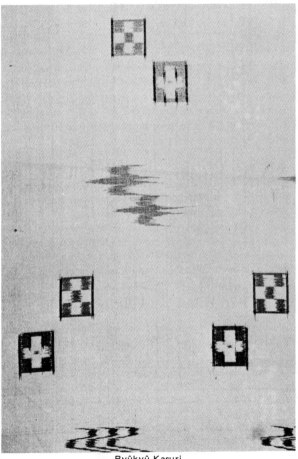

Ryûkyû Kasuri

Where and When to Wear Kimono

Ôburisode

A kimono with sleeves falling to the hem of the skirt is called *ôburisode*. It is the most formal of kimono for young unmarried women. It is embellished with either three or five crests, and the kimono and undergarment are overlapped together as though they were one. A colorful *maru obi* or *fukuro obi* is tied in an elaborate bow. *Ôburisode* are worn by a bride, and they are suitable for any formal affair.

Chûburisode

A kimono with sleeves slightly shorter than those of the *ôburisode* is called *chûburisode,* and it is the next most formal attire. Decorated with either one or three crests, it is tied with an informal *maru obi* or a *fukuro obi* in a magnificent bow. Some *chûburisode* are truly formal while others may be quite simple. Depending upon the color and pattern, *chûburisode* can be worn at weddings, New Year's tea ceremony, and parties. Choose the type for the occasion. *Chûburisode* worn with a sumptuous obi are the usual choice of girls when they wish to dress up.

Koburisode

A short-sleeved *furisode, koburisode,* is equivalent to a colored *tomesode* for young unmarried women. Having five or three crests, it follows the *chûburisode* in degree of formality.

Black Tomesode

The most formal outfit for a married woman, a black *tomesode* is worn at weddings or at any formal congratulatory occasion. It has five dyed crests and a design along the skirt. The usual material is a heavy *hitokoshi chirimen* crepe, but *habutae* and figured satin are also worn. Choose a pattern suitable for your age and preferably one that is not seasonal such as pines, waves, "tortoiseshell" octagons, or fans. The obi is either a *maru obi* or *fukuro obi*. A fan must be carried. It should be gold or silver with bones of black lacquer or ivory.

Colored Tomesode

If a colored *tomesode* has five crests, it can take the place of a black *tomesode*. One with three crests is slightly less formal. As it is worn at formal occasions of a felicitous nature, the patterns are similar to those of the black *tomesode*. It is also worn with a *maru* or *fukuro obi*. A jeweled pin is often attached to a flat *obijime*, but it should be chosen with taste. The fan is the same as above.

Hômongi

Less formal than the *chûburisode* or colored *tomesode*, *hômongi* are lined with a material that is different from the outside. They are worn with a *fukuro obi* or a very good *nagoya obi*. The accessories can be more casual than those that go with the colored *tomesode*. Choose material and colors that suit the kimono. *Hômongi* are worn at tea gatherings, informal parties, New Year's celebrations, or flower exhibitions. The usual fabrics are *hitokoshi* crepe or figured satin, but for an informal change of mood dyed *jôdai omeshi* or *Yûki* are acceptable. The latter are worn by middle-aged women. Because there are all kinds of *hômongi* from formal kimono that are embroidered, tie-dyed, or *yûzen*-dyed to informal batik and *sarasa* prints, you should choose one according to the type of occasion.

Tsukesage

There are also various types of *tsukesage* from informal hand-painted kimono to those with embroidered patterns placed at random over a large area of plain fabric. The latter have a dyed or embroidered crest at the back and usually can be worn like *hômongi*. "*Tsukesage*" indicates a pattern that is especially designed to meet at the top of the shoulders and sleeves so that it will not run upside-down on the opposite side. From the hem at both the front and back the pattern faces toward the top. Patterns both large and small are made.

Komon

Two kinds of *komon* exist: *tsukesage komon* and plain *komon*. If a continuous design, such as fish scales, meets at the top of the kimono instead of running in reverse on the way down the other side, it is classified as *tsukesage komon*. Even though it is a *komon* type, it is a "good" kimono and can be worn for the theater and informal social events as well as for town. As mentioned earlier, small *komon* patterns derive from the stenciled designs used on the formal outfit of Edo Period samurai, but nowadays the term has a much broader use. Any overall pattern large or small, even of *yûzen,* is called *komon.*

Although it is considered best to wear a woven obi with a dyed kimono, a printed *Yûki obi* or, if the design forms a pleasing combination, a printed grosgrain obi or *fukuro nagoya obi* are also in good taste. An over-the-arm handbag is practical. Choose a small one in leather, enamel, or a Japanese style cloth bag. For the *zôri,* enamel is recommended.

Woven Patterns

Omeshi tops this list as it can be worn like a *komon* printed kimono for informal social events, visiting, or going out to the theater. It is comfortable to wear, and for young people there are gay patterns like the "arrow feather" *kasuri* and multi-colored *kasuri*. Some *omeshi* are also made for more formal wear. Other fabrics with woven patterns include such expensive weaves as *Ôshima* (mud-dyed, indigo, white), *Yûki tsumugi* (plain weave, crepe weave), and Ojiya *chijimi*. There are also folk craft regional types of handwoven *tsumugi* and famous *kasuri* like Ryûkyû *kasuri* and Kurume *kasuri*. Kimono made of these fabrics can likewise vary from expensive stylish outfits to house wear. Printed *Yûki* or *jôdai omeshi* can be worn by older women in the manner of *hômongi* if the design is suitable, but no matter how expensive *Ôshima* or *Yûki* may be, they are not appropriate for formal occasions. They are no more than stylish casual clothes. These kimono look best with a printed obi (of ribbed weave or fine crepe) or a *sarasa* pattern.

Wool

Because wool kimono need no lining, they can be sent to the cleaner's without being taken apart. This has naturally led to their growing popularity. For everyday wear at home or in town wool kimono can be arranged in many ways. As a muslin undergarment tends to cling to the kimono, making it difficult to adjust the hem line when the kimono is put on, some slick material like nylon or acetate is a better choice. There are heavy wools for winter and light ones for summer unlined kimono. Wool kimono go well with *fukuro nagoya obi*. Wooden *geta* are worn for everyday, leather or enamel *zôri* for town.

Yukata

Yukata are worn at festivals, for a stroll on a summer evening, or for shopping. Although *nagajuban* or *hanjuban* are not worn with *yukata*, underwear (*hadagi*) of cotton crepe is necessary when going out. The length of the hem and the sleeves is shorter than usual. To give a cool impression, *yukata* are worn rather loose at the neck, but because the cloth wrinkles easily, looking well-dressed in one is not so simple as it may seem.

It is better not to carry a handbag. Instead, put the purse and other things behind the front part of the obi. If a handbag is necessary, it should be something small made of bamboo, vine, or finely plaited palm. When the obi proves too narrow to hold anything safely, a pocket can be sewn on the inside at the front. Because *yukata* look uncomfortable and hot when they are untidy, they should be crisp and neat. *Tabi* are never worn. The feet must therefore be well-manicured. Wear lacquered or bamboo-veneered *geta*.

Haori

As *haori* are not formal wear, they are inappropriate for celebrations, tea ceremony, and the like. But they are not useless. Unlike coats, they can be worn inside a house, to be taken off whenever one feels too warm. For calling on friends to exchange New Year's greetings a *haori* may give a more casual and unassuming impression than appearing with no wrap. At such an occasion the type of patterned *haori* called "*eba haori*" would be proper. A person wearing *haori* can get away with just a makeshift obi. Since that can cause embarrassment if the *haori* has to be taken off, it is wiser always to be correctly dressed.

Eba Haori

Mourning Wear

As explained on p.8, all accessories are in black. The collar is white, or for elderly women black or light grey. In summer plain *ro* gauze or *koma ro* gauze is worn with an unlined *ro* gauze *nagoya obi* in tapestry weave or a figured *ro* gauze or *sha* gauze *nagoya obi*.

Styles of Obi and Methods of Tying

Obi are classified into those for summer use and those for winter use. Of the many kinds that exist, the following are the most common.

Maru Obi

Having a pattern on either side, *maru obi* can be tied in a variety of ways. They go with a bridal costume, a young lady's *furisode*, and black *tomesode*.

Fukuro Obi

This doubleweave obi is for *furisode*, black *tomesode*, colored *tomesode*, or *hômongi*. As the reverse side has no pattern, it is not as versatile as the *maru obi*. There are several kinds from formal to informal.

Nagoya Obi

Nagoya obi come in crepe, ribbed weave, and patterned weaves. Cloth 33 centimeters wide is folded in half to a width of 15 centimeters and backed with a stiffener. This part goes around the waist. The end that forms the "drum" bow is 30 centimeters in width. Besides the drum bow, the only two other ways of tying a *nagoya obi* are the "drum bow variation" (p.107) and the "plover" (p.111).

Fukuro Nagoya Obi

Woven 30 centimeters wide, it is ready to wear as it is. It comes in many qualities from expensive tapestry weave to synthetic or mixed fibers for everyday wear.

Maru Obi   Fukuro Obi   Nagoya Obi   Fukuro Nagoya Obi

Chûya ("Night and Day") Obi

A narrow band of material sewn to a different cloth, this is now worn only as a stylishly casual obi. It is backed with a stiffener.

Hanhaba Obi

This narrow width obi is worn with everyday clothes or under a *haori*.

Odori Obi

Made for stage dancing, this obi is 33 centimeters wide. It is lined, and the outside material is sewn down 2-3 centimeters on the reverse side.

Summer Obi

Maru obi and *fukuro obi* for summer are made of *ro* gauze or *sha* gauze. Unlined obi are of leno weave (*ra*), leno tapestry, tapestry, and *Hakata* weave.

Unlined Nagoya Obi and Summer Nagoya Obi

Unlined *nagoya obi* are of leno weave, *ro* gauze tapestry, and *Hakata* weave. Figured *ro* or *sha* gauze, plain *ro* gauze, or printed ramie are backed with a stiffener. To take advantage of its transparency, *sha* gauze is often backed with a colored stiffener.

Drum Bow Variation

1. As in steps 1 & 2 on p.90, the obi is wrapped around the waist twice. The obi board is inserted, and the obi is securely fastened with the obi clip.
2. The waist pad is put on.
3. At the peak of the "drum" part, make one deep pleat.
4. Without disturbing the pleat, drape the cloth over the bow pad.
5. Put the pad over the clip at a slight slant.
6. Make a fan at the end of the short piece by folding it to about a third its width.
7. Hold the fan arrangement in place with the string of the bow pad. Tie the strings tightly in front.
8. The fan will peek out from behind the drum part of the obi.
9. Put on the *obiage*.

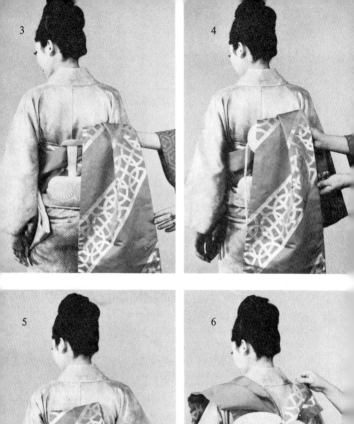
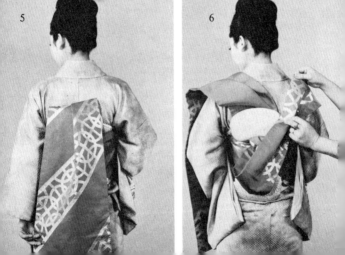

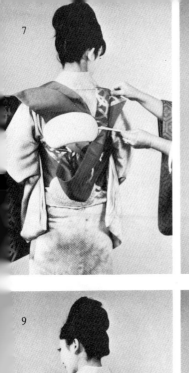

10.11. Arrange the drum part and hold it with an *obijime*.

12. The completed obi. To look girlish, the drum part is made a little smaller than usual. This arrangement is for dress-up occasions.

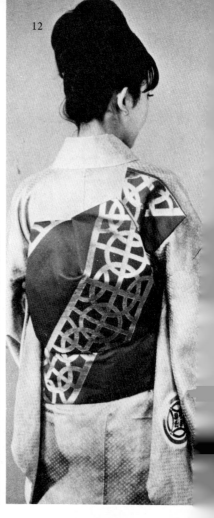

Plover ("Chidori") Bow

1. After following steps 1 & 2 on p.90, make a box pleat at the peak of the drum part.
2. Without disturbing the pleat, drape the cloth over the bow pad.
3. Rest the pad securely on the obi clip.
4. Bring the short end to the upper right.
5. Make three pleats in the middle. This will be a wing.
6. After deciding on how much to show, slip the wing under the bow pad and arrange neatly.

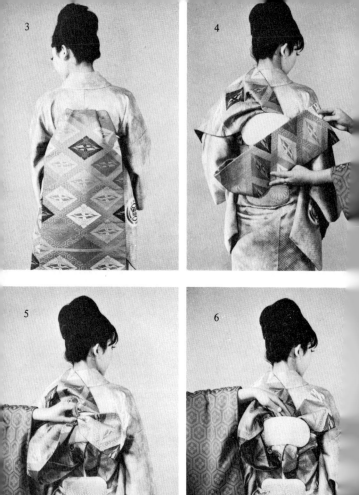

7. Take the base of the short end and pleat it in the same way. Undo the left-hand string of the bow pad, tuck the left wing under it, and arrange it like the wing on the right. Fasten the string again.

8. The two wings completed.

9. Cover the bow pad with the *obiage* and tie in front.

10. Arrange the drum part, fasten with an *obijime*.

11. The finished bow. This is a younger arrangement than the drum bow variation.

9

10

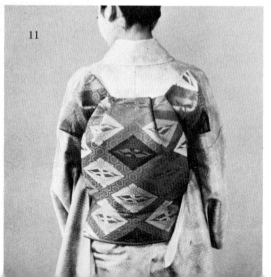

11

114

Ways of Fastening the Obi

(above left)   Twisting
(above right) Tying
(below right) Using an Obi Clip

Regional Weaves

Yonezawa

This weave is made in Yonezawa, Yamagata Prefecture. It was established there 200 years ago when the wise lord of this district, Uesugi Yôzan, commissioned Ojiya experts in crepe weaving to teach in his feudality. A factory was set up within the castle compounds where children of samurai families were taught the techniques of *kasuri* weaving and handspun floss silk. In 1789 a new weave employing reeled silk was manufactured in addition to the crepe, and this continues to this day.

There is a great variety in the types of fabrics produced in Yonezawa: figured kimono material, cloth for *haori*, for padded gowns, and for women's western-style dresses and coats.

Ojiya Chijimi

Because of the heavy snow, no farming can be done in Ojiya, Niigata Prefecture in the winter. Conditions are perfect, however, for the production of ramie yarn which needs a high degree of humidity in the atmosphere. For these reasons, ramie crepe (*chijimi*) and plain ramie (*jôfu*) have become famous products of this area. Both Ojiya *chijimi* and Echigo *jôfu* have been designated Intangible Cultural Assets by the government. Ojiya crepe is made of ramie with a special strongly twisted weft yarn. This gives it a unique crinkled texture that feels pleasantly cool against the skin in the summer.

The history of these fabrics dates back 300 years to the Kanbun Era when a masterless samurai by the name of Hori Jirô arrived in Ojiya accompanied by his wife and daughter. They took up domicile at the house of a local landowner. Jirô had much to teach the country people but he himself was greatly attracted to the ramie cloth woven in the district. Through his efforts to improve it as a summer kimono material, the *kasuri* patterns and the crepe weave were developed.

Tôkamachi

Like Ojiya, Tôkamachi is in Niigata Prefecture and lies buried under deep snow during the winter. It is said that the fabric of Tôkamachi exists because the people must spend half the year enduring the snow. This is an ancient fabric, first made over a thousand years ago from wild ramie that was bleached in the snow. The ramie techniques of crepe that developed in the clear moist air finally also gave rise to a reeled silk known as Akashi *chirimen*. This was a summer material, but since 1925 fabric for printed patterns has also been made. Now products include *omeshi* crepe, Tôkamachi *kasuri*, dyed crepe, and woven patterns for summer.

Kiryû

Kiryû in Gunma Prefecture is a textile center receiving orders from all over Japan. Located only about two hours from Tokyo, it is picturesquely situated near the Oirase and Kiryû Rivers. For its clarity the beautiful Kiryû River is often compared to Kyoto's Kamo River, and in it, too, colorful *yûzen* fabrics are washed. As the whole town is involved in textiles, the clatter of looms can be heard in every direction. The greater part of summer obi produced in Japan come from Kiryû.

The looms of Kiryû have been working for 1,200 years. The

story of how silk came to be woven here goes something like this. When Kiryû was only a village, a local youth fell in love with a maiden who was a lady-in-waiting at the imperial court. Her name was Lady Shirataki. So moving were his poems to her that the emperor was persuaded to allow her to return to Kiryû with him. Together they lived happily raising silk worms and weaving silk. When they had perfected their weaving, they shared their knowledge with the village people. The two are still worshipped as protectors of weaving at Shirataki Shrine in Kiryû.

Chichibu Meisen

As it is blessed with a favorable warm climate, the Chichibu area of Saitama Prefecture has a prosperous sericulture industry. *Meisen* is said to have been first produced here. Known for its fast colors and durability, Chichibu *meisen* is also called *"oni* (demon) *Chichibu."* From the turn of the century it increasingly gained in popularity until reaching a peak in the 1920's. But with the production of wool after the Second World War, *meisen* went into decline, having been replaced by this new material. Chichibu is now trying to re-establish the popularity of *meisen* and recover the position it deserves as originator of this weave.

Murayama Ôshima

This silk *kasuri* made on the outskirts of Tokyo around Shimo Murayama is called Murayama Ôshima. It differs from true Ôshima in that the dyes are chemical. Typical Murayama designs are usually larger and the material wider. Costing about one-third as much as Ôshima, it has made Ôshima style fabrics available to the average consumer. The local young people exhibit an unusual passion for textiles. Planning research trips to other areas or arranging fairs, they are actively involved in the future of Murayama.

Komatsu Satin

A variety of silk fabric, satin (*rinzu*) was introduced from China and was first produced in Japan about 370 years ago at Nishijin in Kyoto. After the war, however, the city of Komatsu has become the center of *rinzu* weaving. Komatsu is located to the southwest of Kanazawa, which has been famous for its silk since the early days of Japanese history. Owing to the encouragement of the Maeda Clan, this area excelled in textiles of the highest quality. Until about 10 years ago, Komatsu satin was ranked among the top three types of kimono material, the other two being *omeshi* and *meisen*.

Satin is either figured or plain. Having a luxuriously smooth, glossy surface, it is made into crested kimono and bedding. Fine satin is used for linings and undergarments. By combining the satin weave with a crepe weave, figured satin is produced. Satin has many uses, being either *yûzen*-printed for kimono and *haori* or dyed in a solid color or black. As a result of present-day demands, Komatsu satin is now also made of synthetic silk and combination synthetic and natural silk fibers.

Iyo Kasuri

The cotton *kasuri* produced in Ehime Prefecture is called Iyo *kasuri*. Its origin is accredited to a woman called Kagiya Kana. When her house was being rethatched, she noticed that wherever the bamboo rafters had been tied, light colored rope designs were left on the dark brown bark. This coincidence prompted her to discover the *kasuri* process.

Upon further experimentation, the fundamentals of Iyo *kasuri* were established. Similar in appearance to Kurume *kasuri*, it has a dark blue ground. The thread is dyed about ten times in vats of natural and chemical indigo until it has become a beautiful deep blue. Both the warp and weft yarns are bound, forming charming patterns. As simple as it is, Iyo *kasuri* is a most attractive weave.

Kurume Kasuri

Woven in the Kurume area of Fukuoka Prefecture, this is a cotton fabric that is said to have been invented 180 years ago by Inoue Den. From the time she was a child, she had had a talent for weaving. One day when she was thirteen, she got the idea of making *kasuri* from her old kimono. Examining the faded spots, she decided to immitate the light and dark areas by tying the yarn before it would be set up on the loom. The result was a dark blue fabric sprinkled with interesting white spots.

So important was this discovery that her story was written up in school books of the early 20th century. Although she later got married, her husband suffered an early death. Continuing to work in textiles all her life, she died at the age of 82. To this day her name is linked with Kurume *kasuri*.

Miyako Jôfu

Miyako ramie comes from two islands, Miyako and Hirara, that lie southwest of Okinawa. The designs are *kasuri* and stripes on an indigo ground. Like Echigo *jôfu*, this handwoven ramie is a luxury summer fabric. Both warp and weft are hand-tied in *kasuri*, and the indigo dye is a local product. After the thread is dried, it is beaten with a mallet. Its characteristic sheen makes it look as though it had been waxed. In fact, some people call it "waxed ramie," but the sheen is caused by a coating of potato starch.

Wool

Nowadays wool is worn for everyday wear or casual visits. Since the introduction of wool, kimono have greatly changed. In former days when a winter kimono became soiled, it had to be taken apart, washed, and resewn – an annoying task. Wool, however, can be sewn by machine and sent to the dry cleaner's in one piece. In the past all kimono other than those for summer were lined to give a little extra warmth to the hand-woven fabric. That wool kimono are quite warm even if unlined has been a prime reason for their popularity.

After the war, Isezaki and Kiryû in Ibaragi Prefecture which had once been foremost producers of *meisen* converted to wool to keep up with popular demands. Even the Nishijin looms that had turned out *omeshi* crepe were set up instead for wool. Now half of the wool production of Japan is from Nishijin. A well-known example of Nishijin wool is Shôzan wool.

GLOSSARY

chijimi: ramie crepe

chirimen: crepe

chûburisode: formal kimono for unmarried women with sleeves falling to just below the knees

datejime: sash or band for fastening the nagajuban and kimono

datemaki: Hakata weave sash for holding the kimono in place

Fuji silk: heavy plain weave silk

fukuro obi: doublecloth obi

furisode: formal kimono with long sleeves for unmarried women

geta: wooden clogs

habutae: lightweight plain silk

hadagi: kimono-style undershirt with short sleeves usually of cotton gauze

Hakata weave: heavy ribbed weave usually of silk

hakama: pleated skirt worn over kimono and paired with haori for men's formal wear

hanjuban: short undergarment worn directly under informal kimono and paired with underskirt of same material

haori: jacket; see p.16 for women, p.20 for men

happi: jacket worn by workmen or participants in festivals; popular in the U.S. as a house coat hitokoshi chirimen: fine silk crepe

hômongi: semi-formal kimono, literally "visit-ing wear"

jôfu: plain ramie

kaku obi: man's stiff obi

kanoko shibori: tie-dye design of small polka dots

kasuri: ikat; design is dyed into yarn before weaving

keisô obi: soft obi for men; or pre-tied obi for women

komon: see p. 32 and p. 100

koshi himo: sashes for fastening undercloths and kimono

kumihimo: braided cord for fastening obi

maruguke: cord covered with silk, used for formal obi

maru obi: formal obi 70 centimeters wide and about 4 meters long

montsuki: formal kimono decorated with family crest

nagajuban: long undergarment worn directly under formal or semi-formal kimono

nagoya obi: see p.104

obiage: piece of fine silk used to conceal bow pad

obijime: cord for fastening obi, especially nagoya obi

obiageshin: pad for holding up obi bow

ôburisode: formal kimono for unmarried women with sleeves falling to hem of kimono

omeshi: see p. 28

Ôshima: see p. 24

otaiko: style of tying obi resembling the taiko drum; called here "drum bow"

ra: leno weave

rinzu: figured satin crepe

ro: gauze weave alternating with plain weave

sarasa: printed patterns deriving from Indian and Indonesian designs

sha: gauze weave

shibori: tie-dye

shioze: heavy faille

susoyoke: underskirt

tabi: split-toed socks

tomesode: see pp. 4 and 5

tsukesage: see p. 7 and p. 100

tsumugi: spun floss silk

yukata: cotton kimono with bold designs

Yûki: see p. 44

yûzen: hand-painted patterns

zôri: thong sandals usually of leather or brocade for women and finely plaited grass for men

HOIKUSHA COLOR BOOKS

ENGLISH EDITIONS

Book Size 4″×6″

COLORED ILLUSTRATIONS FOR NATURALISTS

Text in Japanese, with index in Latin or English.

First Issues (Book Size 6″ × 8″)

1. BUTTERFLIES of JAPAN
2. INSECTS of JAPAN vol.1
3. INSECTS of JAPAN vol.2
4. SHELLS of JAPAN vol.1
5. FISHES of JAPAN vol.1
6. BIRDS of JAPAN
7. MAMMALS of JAPAN
8. SEA SHORE ANIMALS of JAPAN
9. GARDEN FLOWERS vol.1
10. GARDEN FLOWERS vol.2
11. ROSES and ORCHIDS
12. ALPINE FLORA of JAPAN vol.1
13. ROCKS
14. ECONOMIC MINERALS
15. HERBACEOUS PLANTS of JAPAN vol.1
16. HERBACEOUS PLANTS of JAPAN vol.2
17. HERBACEOUS PLANTS of JAPAN vol.3
18. SEAWEEDS of JAPAN
19. TREES and SHRUBS of JAPAN
20. EXOTIC AQUARIUM FISHES vol.1
21. MOTHS of JAPAN vol.1
22. MOTHS of JAPAN vol.2
23. FUNGI of JAPAN vol.1
24. PTERIDOPHYTA of JAPAN
25. SHELLS of JAPAN vol.2
26. FISHES of JAPAN vol.2
27. EXOTIC AQUARIUM FISHES vol.2
28. ALPINE FLORA of JAPAN vol.2
29. FRUITS
30. REPTILES and AMPHIBIANS of JAPAN
31. ECONOMIC MINERALS vol.2
32. FRESHWATER FISHES of JAPAN
33. GARDEN PLANTS of the WORLD vol.1
34. GARDEN PLANTS of the WORLD vol.2
35. GARDEN PLANTS of the WORLD vol.3
36. GARDEN PLANTS of the WORLD vol.4
37. GARDEN PLANTS of the WORLD vol.5
38. THE FRESHWATER PLANKTON of JAPAN
39. MEDICINAL PLANTS of JAPAN

HOIKUSHA
保育社